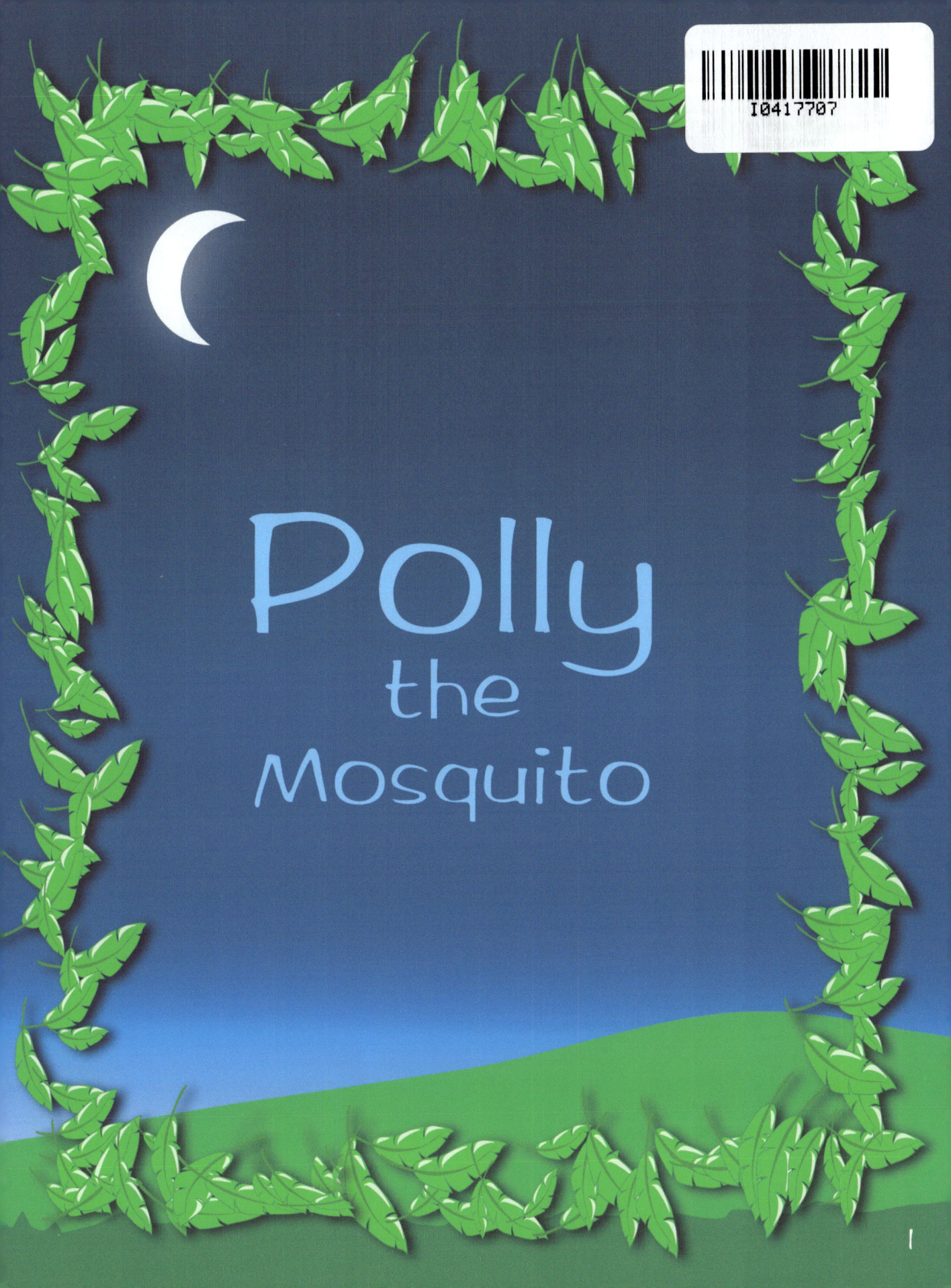

Polly
the
Mosquito

Polly
the
Mosquito

Written by
Veronica Lake

Illustrated by
Scott Merrell

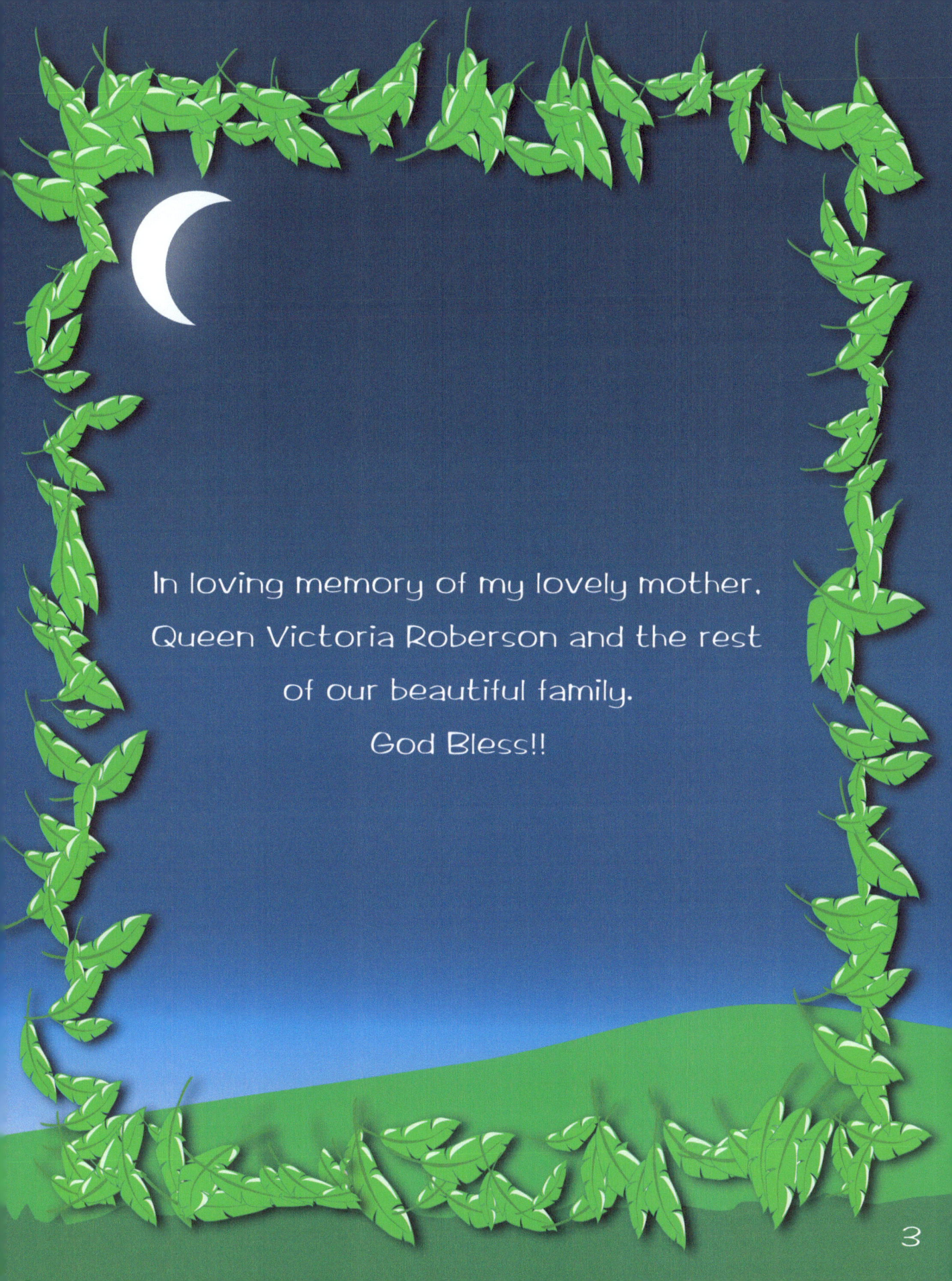

In loving memory of my lovely mother,
Queen Victoria Roberson and the rest
of our beautiful family.
God Bless!!

On a dark, warm, starry night
flew a colony of buzzing mosquitos.

Padre, who was the leader
of the colony announces,
"It's time to teach our
young to sting!"

"To sting?
What do you mean by that?"
asked Polly the youngest
of the colony.

Padre smiled as he
answered, "That's when you
land on the surface of people and
animals and release your stinger
and it really hurts them."

"That's not very nice. I don't think
I would like to learn that" says Polly.

"Come my little ones, it's time to explore!" commanded Padre as the colony came upon a pasture of cows grazing in a field.

Padre whispered quietly,
"Let's teach those old cows a lesson."
"Ouch! Ouch! Ouch"
squealed the cows, as Polly flew
off into the darkness.

"Oh no! Where is Polly?"
Asked the colony.
"Polly. Polly where are you?
Please answer if you hear us."

10

Polly sat quietly in a tree trying
to figure out why does she have to
hurt people and animals when suddenly...

a big spider crept up behind her.
"Yikes!" she shrieked.

As the spider was forming a web,
Polly flew her stinger into him.

The spider quickly squirmed
away as Polly flew off frightened,
yelling "Here I am, here I am!"

"Why did you fly away?" asked Padre.

"Well, I didn't like the idea of hurting anyone, especially if they're not causing you any harm."

"But Polly-" interupted Padre.

Polly quickly interupted. "Let me finish Padre. I had to use my stinger only because I was in danger of being harmed."

"So let's agree, we will only use our stingers for protection" announced Polly.

"Good idea Polly, to be the youngest,
you sure are the smartest."
The colony cheers her on as they fly
off into the night.

19

The End.